537 HILARIOUS TRIVIA QUESTIONS FOR KIDS: QUESTIONS AND ANSWER BOOK FOR KIDS

THE FUNNY FACT AND EASY EDUCATIONAL QUESTIONS Q&A GAME FOR KIDS

JOHNNY NELSON

537 Hilarious Trivia Questions for Kids: Questions and Answer Book for kids by Johnny Nelson Published by BadgerS Publishing

HOW TO PLAY THE GAME

You can teach a student a lesson for a day; but if you can teach him to learn by creating curiosity he will continue the learning process as long as he lives.

— CLAY P. BEDFORD

Reading trivia questions is both fun and educational. It is the best way to enhance intelligence and retention for kids. It's enjoyable to learn while exploring facts across different fields such as animals, science, history, sports and others. It is also a great avenue for family bonding.

Check out the 537 hilarious trivia questions that you can enjoy with your kids. Learning has never been so fun!

HOW TO PLAY THE GAME?

Ask the Question (Q): Consider and form possible answers
Answer (A): Uncover the answer and see if you are correct
or not!

Hint: Keep note of which questions you answer correctly on
a separate piece of paper and compare it with others.

537 Q&A TRIVIA QUESTIONS FOR KIDS

Let's Start...

1. What movie features a toy cowboy named Woody?

Answer: Toy Story

2. Which sailor character would be lost without his can of spinach?

Answer: Popeye

3. Originally, what color was Tweety Bird?

Answer: Pink

4. Before spinach, what did Popeye eat for strength?

Answer: Garlic

5. What is the first name of Pinocchio's cricket friend in the Disney cartoon movie?

Answer: Jiminy

6. Which character was Walt Disney's favorite?

Answer: Goofy

7. Which princess has dyed hair?

Answer: Rapunzel

8. What food makes up nearly all (around 99%) of a Giant Panda's diet?

Answer. Bamboo

9. What was margarine called when it was first marketed in England?

Answer: Butterine

10. What are the two top selling spices in the world?

Answer: Pepper is 1st and mustard is second.

11. Who is the only Disney princess based on a real person?

Answer: Pocahontas

12. In the Disney Pixar movie Monsters Inc., who is the company's best scarer?

Answer: James 'Sully' Sullivan

13. What zoo are the animals from in Madagascar?

Answer: Central Park Zoo

14. What is a baby kangaroo called?

Answer: Joey

15. What is the slowest animal in the world?

Answer: The three-toed sloth

16. What animal does not drink water?

Answer: A kangaroo rat

17. What animal has the male become pregnant and give birth?

Answer: Seahorse

18. Name the seven dwarfs in Snow White?

Answer: Sneezy, Sleepy, Dopey, Doc, Happy, Bashful, Grumpy

19. Who is Shrek's wife?

Answer: Fiona

20. If you are pooped on by this animal, you will supposedly have good luck.

Answer: Bird

21. What's the response to "see you later, alligator?"

Answer: "In a while, crocodile."

22. What type of fish is Nemo?

Answer: A clownfish

23. What is the name of the wooly mammoth in the Ice Age?

Answer: Manfred (Manny)

24. What is the Panda's name in Kung Fu Panda?

Answer: Po

25. What is the name of the vehicle that Scooby Doo and his friends travel in?

Answer: The Mystery Machine

26. Which fruit does Spongebob live in?

Answer: Pineapple

27. Which princess fell in love with a beast?

Answer: Princess Belle

28. What does the score of "love" equal in tennis?

Answer: Zero

29. What television series cartoon dog says, "Ruh Roh!"?

Answer: Scooby Doo

30. Johnny Depp is famously afraid of what?

Answer: Clowns

31. What's Andy's last name in Toy Story?

Answer: Davis

32. Who is the quietest Disney princess?

Answer: Aurora

33. What type of dog is Scooby-Doo?

Answer: Great Dane

34. What does Velma say when she discovers a clue in Scooby-Doo?

Answer: Jinkies

35. In the cartoon world, who has a cousin called Slow-poke Rodriguez?

Answer: Speedy Gonzalez

36. What kind of birds are famous for saying "mine" in Finding Nemo?

Answer: Seagull

37. What planet is home to Chewbacca and the Wookiees in Star Wars?

Answer: Kashyyyk

38. What is Plankton's first name?

Answer: Sheldon

39. What are the names of Donald Duck's three nephews?

Answer: Huey, Dewey, and Louie

40. What does Shaggy say when he's scared in Scooby-Doo?

Answer: Zoinks

41. What is a group of frogs known as?

Answer: army

42. Whose famous line is "Luke, I am your father"?

Answer: Darth Vader

43. What is any human-made object orbiting Earth that no longer serves a useful purpose

Answer: Space Junk

44. What color is the sunset on Mars?

Answer: Blue

45. What is Mr. Krab's full name?

Answer: Eugene H. Krabs

46. What was Mickey Mouse's original name?

Answer: Mortimer Mouse

47. What do the aliens worship as a god in Toy Story?

Answer: The Claw

48. Is tomato a fruit or a vegetable?

Answer: Fruit

49. What kind of squash begins with the letter Z?

Answer: Zucchini

50. What veggie grows on a tall plant that is actually grass?

Answer: Corn on the cob

51. What kind of cat is considered bad luck?

Answer: Black cats

52. What do you call a baby lion?

Answer: A cub

53. In Charlie and the Chocolate Factory, what is Charlie's surname?

Answer: Bucket

54. On the farm, what is a kid?

Answer: A baby goat

55. What Is The Name Of The Cowardly Dog In The Famous Cartoon?

Answer: Courage.

56. Whose nose grew longer every time he lied?

Answer. Pinocchio

57. What Is The Agent Code Of James Bond?

Answer: 007

58. What are the small orange men in Charlie and the Chocolate Factory called?

Answer: Oompa Loompa

59. If a plane crashes on the border between the United States and Canada, where do they bury the survivors?

Answer: Survivors are not buried.

60. What is the major difference between a bird and a fly?

Answer: A Bird can fly but a fly cannot bird!

61. Imagine you are in a sinking rowboat surrounded by sharks. How would you survive?

Answer: Stop imagining

62. If you are in a dark room with a candle, a wood stove and a gas lamp. You only have one match, so what do you light first?

Answer: The match

63. How can a man go eight days without sleep?

Answer: By sleeping during the night

64. Who lives in a trash can on Sesame Street?

Answer: Oscar the Grouch

65. What's the name of the town where The Flintstones live?

Answer: Bedrock

66. What do you call it when a player makes three back to back strikes in bowling?

Answer: Turkey

67. How many rings make up the Olympic rings?

Answer: 5

68. In what sport do you use a wooden ball and mallet?

Answer: Croquet

69. What sport is dubbed the 'king of sports'?

Answer: Soccer

70. What is a baby fox called?

Answer: Kit

71. What kind of animal is Komodo Dragon?

Answer: Lizard

72. What kind of Animal is Abu in Aladdin?

Answer: A monkey

73. What is the name of Mickey Mouse's pet dog?

Answer: Pluto

74. What color are giraffe's tongues?

Answer: Black

75. What do you call a group of giraffes?

Answer: A tower

76. Are worker bees male or female?

Answer: Female

77. What is a group of unicorns known as?

Answer: Blessing

78. What is the literal meaning of the Italian word linguine?

Answer: Little tongues.

79. Where did the pineapple plant originate?

Answer: In South America.

80. What animal has the longest lifespan?

Answer: The Arctic Whale

81. How many legs does a lobster have?

Answer: 10

82. A 'doe' is what kind of animal?

Answer: A female deer

83. Groups of lions are known as what?

Answer: Pride

84. What is the largest type of 'big cat' in the world?

Answer: The tiger

85. If you throw a red stone into the blue sea it will become what?

Answer: It will become wet

86. Why do some cricket players never sweat?

Answer: Because they have huge fans!

87. Bees are found on every continent of the earth except for one, which is it?

Answer: Antarctica

88. Which soft green egg-shaped fruit comes from New Zealand?

Answer. The Kiwi fruit

89. Black-eyed peas are not peas. What are they?

Answer: Beans

90. On what vegetable did an ancient Egyptian place his right hand when taking an oath?

Answer: The onion. Its round shape symbolizes eternity.

91. How many flowers are in the design stamped on each side of an Oreo cookie?

Answer: Twelve. Each has four petals.

92. What is the name of the phobia that involves an abnormal fear of spiders?

Answer: Arachnophobia

93. True or False, dogs can only see in black & white?

Answer: False, dogs can see multiple colors

94. True or false, Dalmatians are born with spots?

Answer: False, Dalmatian puppies are born white and their spots come later in life

95. What are female elephants called?

Answer: Cows

96. Where is the shrimp's head located?

Answer: head

97. What is Mike's last name in *Monsters, Inc.*?

Answer: Wazowski

98. How many noses do slugs have?

Answer: 4

99. What is the only animal that can't jump?

Answer: Elephant

100. A rhinoceros' horn is made of?

Answer: Hair

101. How many glasses of milk can a cow give?

Answer: Nearly 200,000

102. Which direction do bats turn when leaving a cave?

Answer: Left

103. From which country do French fries originate?

Answer: Belgium

104. How many months have 28 days?

Answer: All months.

105. What kind of melon is green on the inside?

Answer: Honeydew

106. What color is blueberry jam?

Answer: Purple

107. What fruit looks like a big orange but is usually pink or yellow in color

Answer: Grapefruit

108. What veggie looks like a bright red potato but is not a potato?

Answer: Beets

109. What food is the most ordered in America?

Answer: Fried chicken

110. Giraffes do not have what organ?

Answer: Vocal cords

111. How many eyes do starfish have?

Answer: eight

112. What is the one that is sticky and brown?

Answer: A stick.

113. What animal can't fart?

Answer: Kangaroos

114. An ostrich eye is bigger than?

Answer: its brain

115. Why can't frogs vomit?

Answer: If frogs have to vomit, they will vomit their entire stomach

116. What animal cannot stick its tongue out?

Answer: Crocodile

117. What animal can't look up into the sky?

Answer: Pigs

118. What beauty products are sometimes made with fish scales?

Answer: Lipstick

119. What fish can blink with both eyes?

Answer: Shark

120. What animal has 32 muscles in each ear?

Answer: Cat

121. What animal has striped skin?

Answer: Tigers. They have striped skin, not just striped fur

122. What animal has the largest eyes in the world?

Answer: Giant squid

123. Bumblebee lives in which country?

Answer: Thailand

124. A male duck is known as what?

Answer: A drake

125. What is the largest land animal?

Answer: African elephant

126. What is a group of crows called?

Answer: A murder

127. How many arms does a starfish have?

Answer: Five

128. What do snakes smell with?

Answer: Their tongue

129. What is the most common training command taught to dogs?

Answer: Sit

130. Do Snakes have eyelids?

Answer: No

131. Can a flying squirrel really fly?

Answer: No

132. The biggest baby in the world belongs to?

Answer: A blue whale

133. What kind of dog is Snoopy?

Answer: Beagle

134. What is the name of Harry Potter's pet owl?

Answer: Hedwig

135. What Group Of Animals Is Collectively Referred To As An Army?

Answer: Frogs

136. How Many Hearts Does An Octopus Have?

Answer: Three

137. What contains more sugar, strawberries or lemons?

Answer: Lemons

138. Can you name the largest chocolate manufacturer in the United States?

Answer: Hershey's

139. A calzone is a type of what?

Answer: Pizza

140. A dried plum is properly known as a?

Answer: Prune

141. Strawberries, raspberries, peaches and cherries are all related to which type of flower?

Answer: Rose

142. From which country do potatoes originate?

Answer: South America

143. What color were the majority of carrots in Europe 400 years ago?

Answer: White carrots

144. In the United States, what are the five most frequently eaten fruits?

Answer: The banana, apple, watermelon, orange, and cantaloupe

145. What was the Teenage Mutant Ninja Turtles' favorite food?

Answer: Pizza

146. What type of oven will not brown foods?

Answer: Microwave oven

147. What animal's milk is used to make authentic Italian mozzarella cheese?

Answer: The water buffalo's

148. What nation produces two thirds of the world's vanilla?

Answer: Madagascar.

149. What is the only fruit to have seeds on the outside?

Answer: Strawberry

150. What veggie is green and looks like a tree?

Answer: Broccoli

151. What fruit do kids traditionally give to teachers?

Answer: An apple

152. What Do You Want The Most When You Feel Thirsty?

Answer: Water

153. What was ice cream called before?

Answer: Cream ice

154. In professional basketball, how high is the basketball hoop from the ground?

Answer: 10 feet

155. What is Canada's national sport?

Answer: Lacrosse

156. How many Olympic games were held in countries that no longer exist?

Answer: 3

157. Before 1894, basketball games were played with what sort of ball?

Answer: Soccer ball

158. Which country does footballer Lionel Messi play for?

Answer: Argentina

159. Crawl, backstroke, and butterfly are different methods in which sport?

Answer: Swimming

160. Which chess piece can only move diagonally?

Answer: The Bishop

161. What is the name of the Australian throwing stick that can return to its thrower?

Answer: Boomerang

162. What term is used in tennis for 40-40?

Answer: Deuce

163. Ping-pong is an alternative name for which sport?

Answer: Table Tennis

164. In which sport might you do a slam dunk?

Answer: Basketball

165. What is the most expensive property on a standard British monopoly board?

Answer: Mayfair

166. Do you know what the first puck used in ice hockey made of?

Answer. Frozen cow dung

167. What sport's hall of fame enshrined Abraham Lincoln for having a stellar record of just one loss?

Answer: Wrestling

168. What was the first animal to go into orbit?

Answer: A dog

169. What was the name of the first animal to go into orbit?

Answer: Laika

170. Earth is located in which galaxy?

Answer: The Milky Way Galaxy

171. Which planets in the Solar System are known as the Gas Giants?

Answer: Jupiter, Saturn, Uranus and Neptune

172. Is the sun a star or a planet?

Answer: A star

173. What is the name of NASA's most famous space telescope?

Answer: Hubble Space Telescope

174. What is the name of Saturn's largest moon?

Answer: Titan

175. What is the name of the first satellite sent into space?

Answer: Sputnik

176. Which planet has craters named after famous artists, musicians, and authors?

Answer: Mercury

177. What flavor ice cream did Baskin-Robbins release to celebrate America's landing on the moon?

Answer: Lunar Cheesecake

178. Which planet is named after the Roman goddess of beauty?

Answer: Venus

179. What is the name of the largest peak on Mars?

Answer: Olympus Mons

180. From which language did the word "Ketchup" come?

Answer: Chinese

181. Which planet is famous for its great red spot?

Answer: Jupiter

182. What was the first fruit that was eaten on the moon?

Answer: Peach

183. What is the slowest animal in the world?

Answer: Sloth

184. A snail can sleep for how many years?

Answer: 3 years

185. Which animal never sleeps?

Answer: A bullfrog

186. What is a baby fox called?

Answer: A kit

187. What animal does not drink water?

Answer: A kangaroo rat

188. What is the coldest place in the universe?

Answer: The Boomerang Nebula

189. What is the largest type of star in the universe?

Answer: Red supergiant stars

190. What is the name of Alice's cat in Alice in Wonderland?

Answer: Dinah

191. What word does the owl use to describe falling in love in Bambi?

Answer: Twitterpated

192. Mary Poppins' umbrella has what type of animal at the end of the handle?

Answer: A talking parrot

193. What movie is the song "Heigh-Ho"?

Answer: Snow White and the Seven Dwarfs

194. Which Disney princess disguises herself as a man?

Answer: Mulan

195. Which princess has a raccoon as a companion?

Answer: Pocahontas

196. Who and what is the nursemaid to the children in Peter Pan?

Answer: Nanna, a Saint Bernard dog

197. Harry Potter plays which wizarding sport on broomsticks?

Answer: Quidditch

198. Who is the golfer whose first name is the same as that of a big cat?

Answer: Tiger Woods

199. What swimming stroke has the same name as a flying insect?

Answer: Butterfly

200. What is it that players hit in badminton?

Answer: Shuttlecock

201. What is the wood-carver's name in Pinocchio?

Answer: Geppetto

202. What famous cola company featured a smiling Santa on their products?

Answer: Coca-Cola

203. What snack is left for Santa on Christmas Eve?

Answer: Milk and cookies

204. What animal has the longest lifespan?

Answer: The arctic whale

205. How many legs does a lobster have?

Answer: 10

206. Can an ostrich fly?

Answer: No

207. What is the only thing Alvin wants for Christmas?

Answer: A hula-hoop

208. What do people do under the mistletoe?

Answer: Kiss

209. In, How the Grinch Stole Christmas, what three words are used to describe the Grinch?

Answer: Stink, stank, stunk

210. If you were to take Elmo with you to an Independence Day party, what would he love the most?

Answer: The Fireworks

211. What is the most popular food that Americans eat on Independence Day?

Answer: Hotdogs

212. What language has three genders?

Answer: German: masculine, feminine, and neuter

213. What language consists entirely of whistles?

Answer: La Gomera

214. What was the first language spoken in outer space?

Answer: Russian

215. In The Simpsons what is the name of the cat?

Answer: Snowball

216. What is the most spoken language in the world?

Answer: Mandarin Chinese

217. What is the official language of airplane travel?

Answer: English

218. What sentence has all the letters in the English alphabet?

Answer: The quick brown fox jumps over the lazy dog

219. What is the only word with double 'i'?

Answer: Skiing

220. Can you tell which vowel is not found in the word nine hundred ninety-nine?

Answer: a

221. What is the only 15-letter word that can be spelled without a repeating letter?

Answer: Uncopyrightable

222. What do you call the dot over the letter 'i'?

Answer: title

223. What is the shortest sentence in the English language that consists of one word?

Answer: Go

224. Where was the hamburger made?

Answer: Connecticut

225. What is the world's popcorn capital?

Answer: Indiana

226. What is the magic capital of the world?

Answer: Michigan

227. What U.S. state houses the city that is the ice cream capital of the world?

Answer: Iowa.

228. Which state was the fortune cookie actually invented?

Answer: California, San Francisco

229. Chug, chug, chug, Puff, puff, puff is how which famous book begins?

Answer: The Little Engine That Could.

230. What was the last name of Buzz who appeared in Toy Story?

Answer: Lightyear.

231. What was the name of the caped crusader who operated in Gotham city?

Answer: Batman.

232. What cartoon character is always saying "what's up doc"?

Answer: Bugs Bunny

233. What Washington Irving character fell asleep for 20 years?

Answer: Rip Van Winkle

234. What State is famous for Disneyland and Hollywood?

Answer: California

235. Which state was the 50th state to join the union?

Answer: Hawaii.

236. What was the name of Clark Kent's high school sweetheart?

Answer: Lana Lang.

237. Mickey Mouse has how many fingers on each hand?

Answer: Four.

238. What was the name of the restaurant Doc Hopper wanted to open in The Muppet Movie?

Answer: Frogs' Legs.

239. What comes after a million, billion, & trillion?

Answer: Quadrillion

240. Which science is the study of rocks?

Answer: Geology

241. What color is given to the second full moon of the month?

Answer: Blue

242. The left side of your body is controlled by which side of your brain?

Answer: The right side of the brain

243. After which animal are the Canary Islands named?

Answer: Dogs

244. What kind of animal is the firefly?

Answer: It's a winged beetle.

245. What color is a purple finch?

Answer: Raspberry red

246. What kind of animal is a prairie dog?

Answer: Rodent

247. What kind of animal is the horned toad?

Answer: A lizard

248. What vegetable can make you turn orange?

Answer: Carrots

249. What happens to our eyes when we sneeze?

Answer: They close.

250. In the nursery rhyme, where did the old lady with too many kids live?

Answer: In a shoe

251. Which animal is known as the 'Ship of the Desert'?

Answer: A camel

252. What type of mythical animal did St. George, the patron saint of England, slay?

Answer: A dragon

253. What is Harry Potter's middle name?

Answer: James

254. What is the female smurf called?

Answer: Smurfette

255. What is another name for green apple?

Answer: Granny Smith

256. Winnie the Pooh lived where?

Answer: Hundred Acre Wood.

257. In The Simpsons what is the name of the cat?

Answer: Snowball.

258. What cartoon character's first name is Quincy?

Answer: Mr. Magoo.

259. What is the name of the shrunken city in a bottle in the Superman comics?

Answer: Kandor

260. What English word becomes its opposite when the letters FE are in front of it?

Answer. Male

261. You catch a fish, a cold, and your breath. What do you do to a street, your heart, and swords?

Answer. Cross

262. The name of a well-known American actress contains the five vowels (A,E,I,O,U) exactly once, though not in that order. The consonants in her name are B,J,L,R,S, and T (not in that order). Who is she?

Answer. Julia Roberts

263. Name the only book William Shakespeare ever wrote?

Answer. The Complete Works of William Shakespeare

264. Who wrote The Autobiography of Mark Twain?

Answer. Mark Twain

265. In 'Finding Nemo', what is Nemo's dad called? Marvin, Marlin or Martin?

Answer: Marlin

266. Which country gave us the words 'shampoo' and 'pyjamas'?

Answer: India

267. What is the name of the new villain of Iron Man 3? The Mandarin, The Marvellin or The Mandible?

Answer: The Mandarin

268. If a carnivore eats meat, what does a frugivore eat?

Answer: frugivore is a fruit eater.

269. In the Disney movie 'Frozen', what is the name of the snowman that comes to life?

Answer: Olaf

270. In the movie Madagascar 3, what do Alex and the gang join?

Answer: A travelling circus

271. What is the name of Garfield the cat's owner?

Answer: John

272. What does a podiatrist specialize in?

Answer: Feet

273. What is the name of the bright green frog that stars in the muppets?

Answer: Kermit

274. SpongeBob started the interview off by asking Mario, "Where do you live?" What response did Mario give to this question?

Answer: The Mushroom Kingdom

275. This is a series about a feline and canine that share a body. What was it called?

Answer: CatDog

276. Where do SpongeBob SquarePants and his friends live?

Answer: Bikini Bottom

277. In the episode "Life of Crime" what color is the balloon Spongebob and Patrick "borrow"?

Answer: Red

278. What is the only number spelled out in English that has the same number of letters as its value?

Answer: Four

279. Bananas are part of what family?

Answer: Berries

280. Ice cream mixed with soda is referred to as what?

Answer: A float

281. According to legend, vampires are exceptionally vulnerable to which vegetable?

Answer: Garlic

282. On "Hey Arnold," what is Curly's last name?

Answer: Gamelthorp

283. What was the original flavor of the filling in Twinkies?

Answer: Banana cream

284. What is a group of ravens known as?

Answer: Unkindness

285. What is a group of crows called?

Answer: Murder

286. How many bones do sharks have?

Answer: 0

287. A snail can sleep for how many years?

Answer: 3

288. In Disney cartoons, what was Goofy's nephew's name?

Answer: Gilbert

289. In the cartoon series the Flintstones where was Pebbles born?

Answer: Rockapedic Hospital.

290. What number is a baker's dozen?

Answer: 13

291. What animal produces pink milk?

Answer: Hippopotamus

292. What is the shape of a goat's pupil?

Answer: rectangle

293. Without what insect, there would be no Chocolate?

Answer: Flies

294. You can make diamonds from what food?

Answer: Peanut Butter

295. Where do Kim Possible and her family live?

Answer: Middleton

296. What African country was the first ever to qualify for a World Cup?

Answer: Egypt

297. In China, animals are forbidden to use human language. This belief led to the ban of a book of which famous writer, in the country?

Answer: Lewis Carol

298. Which basketball player was Michael Jordan nick-named after as a young high school basketball enthusiast?

Answer: Magic after Magic Johnson

299. If you hug a 'guling', are you hugging an animal, a toy or a pillow?

Answer: If you hug a 'guling' you are hugging a pillow.

300. The 'oval pigtoe' is a type of crab, snake or mussel?

Answer: The 'oval pigtoe' is a type of freshwater mussel.

301. What other animal purrs like cats do?

Answer: Elephant

302. What animal cannot stick out their tongue?

Answer: Crocodiles

303. What animal breathes through their skin?

Answer: Salamander

304. Beefsteak is a variety of what fruit?

Answer: Tomato

305. What color is a rhubarb?

Answer: Red

306. The Tour de France is what kind of race?

Answer: Bicycle

307. What is a group of toads known as?

Answer: knot

308. Which of the following characters in "The Power-puff Girls" has the ability to speak Spanish?

Answer: Bubbles

309. In the word pretty, the E is pronounced like a short I. In women, the O is pronounced like a short I. In what familiar 4-letter word is U pronounced like a short I?

Answer. Busy

310. Name a part of the body that begins with the letter L. Change the L to T and, phonetically, you'll name another part of the body. What is it?

Answer. Tongue, Lung

311. What is the cross between a donkey and a zebra known as?

Answer: Zeedonk

312. What was the original world for butterfly?

Answer: Flutterby

313. If you boil beetroot in water, and then massage the water into your scalp each night, it works as an effective cure for what?

Answer: Dandruff

314. In the United States, what is the second most popular fresh vegetable.

Answer: Lettuce

315. Onion is Latin for what?

Answer: Large pearl

316. What is the only food that will never rot and can last 3000 years?

Answer: Honey

317. What is the most stolen food in the world?

Answer: Cheese

318. What fruit bounce like a rubber ball when ripe?

Answer: Cranberries

319. In 2001, there were more than 300 banana-related accidents in Britain, most involving people slipping on skins. True or false?

Answer: True

320. Eating a lot of beetroot turns your pee into what color?

Answer: Pink

321. Lettuce is a member of what family?

Answer: Sunflower

322. What fruit can be used as blood plasma?

Answer: Coconut water

323. Who composed the music for Sonic the Hedgehog 3?

Answer: Michael Jackson

324. What can't a cheetah do that a tiger and a puma can do?

Answer: Retract its claws

325. Cockroaches do what every fifteen minutes?

Answer: Fart

326. What is the name of the breakfast cereal produced by World Wrestling Entertainment (the WWE)?

Answer: Booty O's

327. If one is wearing a swimsuit in Florida in public, what is illegal for one to do?

Answer: Sing

328. In Alaska it's legal to shoot bears, but not allowed to do what?

Answer: Wake one up

329. When people are frightened their ears produce more of what?

Answer: Earwax

330. Footprints and tire tracks left behind by astronauts on the moon will not stay there forever. True or False?

Answer: False. They will stay forever as there is no wind to blow them away

331. What is the only planet that rotates on its side like a barrel?

Answer. Uranus

332. Most of the dust in your home is actually what?

Answer: Dead skin

333. A hippopotamus is huge so it cannot run faster than a man. True or False?

Answer: False

334. Even if an analog clock is broken, at least it shows the correct time twice a day. True or False?

Answer: True

335. What is impossible with your eyes open?

Answer: Sneezing

336. What is the trickiest tongue twister in the English language?

Answer: "Sixth sick sheik's sixth sheep's sick".

337. 90% of the world's freshwater is in what continent?

Answer: Antarctica

338. What is the largest desert in the world?

Answer: Antarctica

339. There are no polar bears in Antarctica. True or False?

Answer. True, they are in the Arctic!

340. What is the only place in the world that has only one ATM?

Answer: Antarctica

341. Less than 200 languages are spoken in Europe. True or False?

Answer: False. Over 200 languages are spoken in Europe

342. What is the largest country in Europe?

Answer: Russia!

343. What is the smallest country in Europe?

Answer. Vatican

344. What is the most visited place in Europe? It is also known as the happiest place on Earth.

Answer: Disneyland

345. Where is Disneyland in Europe?

Answer: Disneyland is in Paris!

346. No pig is allowed to be called what name in France?

Answer: Napoleon

347. The largest island in the world is what?

Answer: Green Land

348. What are the only two countries in Africa that were not colonised by the European powers?

Answer: Ethiopia and Liberia

349. What is the only country that can't join FIFA because of bad weather conditions and grass can not grow there?

Answer: Greenland

350. In what country is selling, importing or spitting out chewing gum is illegal?

Answer: Singapore

351. What is the driest place on Earth?

Answer: Antarctica

352. In what country can you visit Machu Picchu?

Answer: Peru

353. Which African nation has the most pyramids?

Answer: Sudan

354. What African country served as the setting for Tatooine in Star Wars?

Answer: Tunisia

355. What is Donald Duck's sister's name?

Answer: Dumbella.

356. Who are Daisy Duck's three nieces?

Answer. April May June

357. In Peanuts, where was Snoopy born?

Answer: Daisy Hill Puppy Farm.

358. What % of an egg's weight is the shell?

Answer: approx 12%.

359. Which is the most eaten food in the world?

Answer: Rice.

360. A dog is a canine. What is a bear?

Answer: A ursine.

361. In Quitman Georgia it's not allowed for a chicken to do what?

Answer: Cross the Road

Difficult Funny Trivia **Questions for Kids**

362. On average, how many times do you fart per day?

Answer: 14

363. What was the first food eaten in space?

Answer: Applesauce

364. What is the fear of ducks watching you?

Answer: Anatidaephobia

365. What is the world record for the number of hotdogs eaten in one sitting?

Answer: 74

366. What is the love for eating ice called?

Answer: Pagophagia

367. Some perfumes have what kind of poo?

Answer: Whale

368. What is the name of the first pizzeria to open in the United States?

Answer: Lombardi's Pizza

369. On what planet does it rain metal?

Answer: Venus

370. What is the hardest to pronounce town?

Answer: Llanfairpwllgwyngyllgogerychwyrndrobwyll llantysiliogogogoc

371. Which Indian Athlete Is Known As The Flying Sikh Of India?

Answer: Milkha Singh.

372. During the first-ever modern Olympics, what were the first placers awarded with?

Answer: Silver medals

373. What is a small country in the Middle East that is made up of vowels and consonants? It is also the longest name of a country whose letters do that.

Answer: United Arab Emirates

374. What is the shortest word in English that has letters a, b, c, d, e, and f?

Answer: Feedback

375. What is the longest English word without any

vowel?

Answer: Rhythms

376. What is the only common word in English that has five vowels in a row?

Answer: Queueing

377. In 2012, which toy was sent up over 24,000 meters towards the edge of space by two Canadian students using a weather balloon?

Answer: A lego man

378. What is the latin name for polar bear?

Answer: Sea bear

379. When was the first selfie taken?

Answer: 1839

380. What is the longest word in English that has 45 letters?

Answer: pneumonoultramicroscopicsilicovolcanokoniosis

381. What English word has 464 definitions?

Answer: set

382. Ever since World War Two, what beverage's equipment is furnished in British battle tanks?

Answer: Tea

383. Victorians said this word before having their picture taken instead of the word "cheese". What fruit did they say?

Answer: Prunes

384. What natural human bodily fluid did Romans use as mouth wash because of the presence of ammonia in it?

Answer: Urine

385. The United State of America's Statue of Liberty was a gift from which European Country?

Answer: France

386. A snow crystal has how many sides?

Answer: Six:

387. How many legs does a fly have?

Answer: Six.

388. What is an Australian parakeet called?

Answer: A budgerigar.

389. How many eyes does an earthworm have?

Answer: None.

390. What is a seven-letter word in English that consists of ten words without rearranging any letters?

Answer: therein

391. What is the longest word in the English language with all letters in alphabetical order?

Answer: Almost

392. In Swedish what is "entrance" and "driveway"?

Answer: "Infart" and "Uppfart."

393. Who wrote the children's book Gangsta Granny?

Answer: David Walliams

394. How long is the longest movie ever made?

Answer: Cure for Insomnia

395. What is the length of the longest movie ever?

Answer: 85 hours

396. What is the fear of long words known as?

Answer: Hippopotomostrosesquippedaliophobia

397. Washington police officers get a half hour class in how to what?

Answer: Sit Down

398. What is the only species of bird that can fly backward?

Answer: A hummingbird

399. A third of the world's languages are spoken in what continent?

Answer: Africa

400. Coffee is grown commercially in what US state?

Answer: Hawaii

401. After Christianity, what is the 2nd largest Religion in the U.S.A?

Answer: Judaism

402. Which animal blows up like a balloon when it feels threatened?

Answer: Pufferfish

403. Which species of bear has a translucent fur?

Answer: Polar Bear

404. Which animal is the largest in the squirrel family?

Answer: Groundhog

405. Besides humans, what is the only primate capable of having blue eyes?

Answer: Black Lemur

406. What is the fastest two-legged land animal?

Answer: The ostrich

407. What animal is considered the world's largest rodent?

Answer: The capybara

408. In Florida only on Sundays, it is not allowed for a single woman to do what?

Answer: Skydive

409. In California you can't buy a mousetrap without having what?

Answer: A hunting license

410. In Georgia, you are not allowed to eat what with a fork?

Answer: Fried chicken

411. In Minnesota you are not allowed to tease what type of animal?

Answer: Skunks

412. In June in Wyoming you are not allowed to take a picture of what?

Answer: A rabbit

413. What is illegal to eat with a cherry pie in Kansas?

Answer: Ice cream

414. In Michigan, you are not allowed to chain what animal to a fire hydrant?

Answer: An Alligator

415. What is the oldest of the seven wonders of the Ancient world that is still in existence?

Answer: The Pyramid of Giza

416. What is the official animal of Scotland?

Answer: Unicorn

417. How many people visit the Great Wall of China every year?

Answer: 10 million

418. What country has the highest rate of twin births in the world?

Answer: Nigeria

419. What is the most endangered island nation?

Answer: The Marshall Islands

420. What is the oldest state in the world?

Answer: San Marino

421. How many times are Americans injured in the toilet per year?

Answer: 40,000

422. What movie has an animated character that has the name of a vegetable and is forced to live in a foster home?

Answer: My Life as a Zucchini

423. In Texas, you are not allowed to say bad words in front of a what?

Answer: Corpse

424. In South Dakota, you are not allowed to fall down and sleep where?

Answer: In a Cheese Factory

425. What ailment kills the most fruit flies?

Answer: Constipation

426. What animal sleeps up to 22 hours each day?

Answer: Koala

427. Which dinosaur had 15 horns?

Answer: Kosmoceratops

428. What is the feminine of a cat?

Answer: Queen

429. What is the heaviest spider in the world?

Answer: Goliath Birdeater Tarantula

430. Which animal is the only one in the world with an odd number of whiskers?

Answers: A catfish

431. How many pairs of eyelids does an owl have?

Answers: 3

432. Which snake is the only one known to build a nest?

Answers: A king cobra

433. It's illegal in Texas to put what on your neighbors Cow?

Answer: Graffiti

434. In Connecticut, a pickle must do what to be legal?

Answer: Bounce

435. In Vermont, women can't wear what without written permission from their husbands?

Answer: False Teeth

436. What did people in the Middle Ages throw at the bride and groom?

Answer: Eggs

437. In what country would one compete in a "wife carry race"?

Answer: Finland

438. What sport has been played on the moon?

Answer: Golf

439. What is a haboob?

Answer: A type of sandstorm

440. What is the number one seller at Walmart?

Answer: Bananas

441. In Equatorial Guinea, what are you not allowed to name your child?

Answer: Monica

442. 33% of the world's population can't do what with their fingers?

Answer: Snap their fingers

443. With what did the ancient Romans dye their hair?

Answer: Bird poop

444. What Is The Name Of The Oldest Football Club In India?

Answer: Mohun Bagan A.C.

445. In football, who was nicknamed 'The Divine Ponytail'?

Answer: Roberto Baggio

446. What country has competed the most times in the Summer Olympics without winning a gold medal?

Answer: The Philippines

447. What razor-thin country accounts for more than half of the western coastline of South America?

Answer: Chile

448. Mercury has many craters on its surface. Which is the largest in diameter?

Answer: Caloris Basin

449. What is the longest word in English that contains only vowels?

Answer: Euouae

450. What are the words that contain all six vowels in alphabetical order?

Answer: "facetiously," "abstemiously," and "arseniously"

451. What is the word that contains all five vowels in reverse alphabetical order?

Answer: "duoliteral"

452. What is the longest word in English that does not contain the letter "e"?

Answer: Floccinaucinihilipilification,

453. In Ohio, by law, all pets have to carry what at night?

Answer: Lights on their tails

454. In Oklahoma City a prisoner is not allowed to wear what?

Answer: Pink Bikini Underwear

455. What place has coins that feature Disney and "Star Wars" characters?

Answer: Niue, an island nation in the South Pacific

456. What country follows a calendar that is seven years behind the rest of the world?

Answer: Ethiopia

457. In what country can you marry a dead person?

Answer: France

458. What country has the most natural lakes?

Answer: Canada

459. In what country do the authorities ban its people from wearing yellow clothing?

Answer: Malaysia

460. What is the only sea without any coasts?

Answer: Sargasso Sea

461. In Massachusetts, you are not allowed to have what in the bathroom?

Answer: A light switch

462. In Alaska, you are not allowed to look at a moose from where?

Answer: The window of any aircraft

463. In which Tennessee city it is not allowed to lasso fish?

Answer: Knoxville

464. The pumpkin originated in which country about 9,000 years ago?

Answer: Mexico

465. Although the Stegosaurus dinosaur was over 9 metres long, its brain was only the size of what?

Answer: A walnut

466. Humans get a little taller in space because there is no gravity pulling down on them. True or False?

Answer: True

467. Because of the unusual shape of their legs, what Australian animals struggle to walk backwards?

Answer: kangaroos and emus

468. Square watermelons sell for about how much?

Answer: 85 dollars

469. How old was the youngest US mayor?

Answer: 3-years-old

470. What is the tip of a shoelace called?

Answer: Aglet

471. What is the blob of toothpaste that sits on your toothbrush called?

Answer: Nurdle

472. What is the smelliest flower?

Answer: rafflesia

473. Instead of apples what do Adams family members bob for?

Answer: Crabs

474. In what country is it considered good luck if a coconut is cleanly split open without jagged edges?

Answer: Philippines

475. What type of animal is an imbabala?

Answer: Antelope

476. What is the longest English word with only one vowel?

Answer: Strengths

477. Unless one is a magician, what are you not allowed to own as a pet in Queensland, Australia?

Answer: A rabbit

478. What is the main ingredient of Bombay Duck?

Answer: Fish

479. Who said: "I'm the president of the United States and I'm not going to eat any more broccoli"?

Answer: George Bush

480. The Dunkin' Donuts in South Korea offer doughnut flavors such as Kimchi Croquette and Glazed Garlic. True or False?

Answer: True

481. Jupiter's 4 biggest moons are named what?

Answer: Europa, Ganymede, Callisto and Io

482. Hawaii is moving towards what country at the speed of 10 cm a year?

Answer: Japan because they are on different tectonic plates

483. What animals can see behind themselves without even moving their heads?

Answer: Rabbits and parrots

484. What animal tastes food by standing on top of it?

Answer: Butterflies. Their taste receptors are in their feet unlike humans who have most on their tongue

485. How many flowers must Honeybee workers visit to make one pound of honey?

Answer: 2 million

486. The fear of vegetables is called?

Answer: Lachanophobia

487. Mount Kilimanjaro is the highest mountain of which continent?

Answer: Africa

488. NASA has said that soil on Mars might be good for growing what?

Answer: Turnips

489. What substance is a rhino horn made of?

Answer: Hair

490. Which bird only eats bones?

Answer: The bearded vulture

491. What is the smallest reptile in the world?

Answer: A leaf chameleon

492. What is the world's most poisonous spider?

Answer: The Brazilian

493. How many legs does a honey bee have?

Answer: 6

494. How many glasses of milk does a cow give in its life?

Answer: 200,000

495. Only two mammals lay eggs. Which ones?

Answer: The spiny anteater and the duck-billed platypus

496. What kind of creature is a Portuguese man-of-war?

Answer: A jellyfish

497. What type of animal is an Impala?

Answer: A cob

498. What is the heaviest species of monkey?

Answer: The mandrill

499. A cow's stomach has how many compartments?

Answer: 4

500. Which African animal's name literally means "water horse"?

Answer: A hippopotamus

501. Which animal can rotate their head 270 degrees?

Answer: An owl

502. What is Scotland's national animal?

Answer: The unicorn

503. What does the word Matrix mean in the Bible?

Answer: Womb

504. By what name is the California Poppy flower also known as?

Answer: Cup of gold

505. How many times of its own weight can an ant pull?

Answer: Around ten times.

506. Our body contains gold. Which body part has the most gold in it?

Answer: The toe nails.

507. Which animal runs faster than a horse, and can live longer than a camel without water?

Answer: A giraffe.

508. What is the most common cause of plane accidents?

Answer: Birds getting sucked into the plane's engine.

509. Which animal stands on its feet for the longest time?

Answer: The African elephant. Around 50 years. It even sleeps standing up.

510. The space between your nostrils is called a what?

Answer: A columella

511. Large groups of what nuts can spontaneously combust?

Answer: Pistachios

512. You can't overcook what food?

Answer: Mushrooms

513. Most animals have just two of these, but an iguana has three! What is it?

Answer: Eyes

514. What is the smallest alphabet?

Answer: The Papuan language of Rotokas

515. How old is the world's oldest piece of chewing gum?

Answer: 9,000 years old

516. In what language does "air" mean water?

Answer: Indonesian

517. How many noses does a slug have?

Answer: Four

518. How much can one person eat in a year?

Answer: 2,000 pounds of food.

519. What animal can sleep standing up?

Answer: Cow

520. In North Carolina it is not allowed to use what to plough cotton fields?

Answer: Elephants

521. What did J Edgar Hoover stop people from walking on?

Answer: His Shadow

522. According to doctors, people with what kind of pets fall asleep the easiest?

Answer: Fish

523. By law what is it against the law to do in Minnesota with your washing line?

Answer: Mix male and female washing together

524. A P Herbert, editor of Punch, once wrote a check on what?

Answer: The side of a cow.

525. According to Massachusetts law, what can you not do to a pigeon?

Answer: Scare it

526. In Hartford Connecticut it is not allowed to educate what?

Answer: Your dog

527. Where is it illegal to carry old chewing gum stuck on your nose?

Answer: In Somalia

528. In the 18th century what job did a fart-catcher do?

Answer: A footman who walked behind the Master

529. Pope John XX1 used what was effective eyewash?

Answer: Babies Urine

530. By law, in Louisiana, who cannot be charged more than twenty five cents for a haircut?

Answer: Bald Men

531. When held to ultraviolet light, what animal's urine glows in the dark?

Answer: Cat

532. How many pounds of food does Hollywood superstar Dwayne "the Rock" Johnson consume daily?

Answer: 10

533. Which bird's nostrils are at the end of its beak?

Answer: The Kiwi.

534. Which insect has the best eyesight amongst all?

Answer: The dragonfly.

535. The hippopotamus belongs to which family or species?

Answer: The pig.

536. What is the lead in pencil made from?

Answer: Not from lead like we all think. It is made from a mix of clay and graphite.

537. The place that cartoon characters store things, just to pull out of thin air, is known as?

Answer: Hammerspace

538. What is Oklahoma's state vegetable?

Answer: Watermelon

539. One of the most popular pizza toppings in what country is green peas?

Answer: Brazil

540. The winner of the 2013 Nathan's Hot Dog Eating contest consumed 69 hot dogs in how many minutes?

Answer: 10 minutes

541. Almonds are a member of what family?

Answer: The peach family

AHA! 541! Surprised you with some bonuses, didn't I?

A THOUGHT TO LEAVE ON

Thank you for playing our Q&A Game. Learning retention games are very beneficial to children's educational development. That is what we pride ourselves in bringing to you.

We suggest revisiting this book every 3 months or so and seeing how much of it can be recalled. You will be amazed at how the repetition of this exercise can benefit the recall ability of the human brain in any situation.

Don't just teach your kids to read, teach them to question what they read. Teach them to question everything.

— GEORGE CARLIN

Made in United States
North Haven, CT
19 August 2022